A Study of 1, 2, 3 John

ABIDING IN LOVE

William Carter

Abingdon Press / Nashville

ABIDING IN LOVE
A STUDY OF 1, 2, 3 JOHN

Scripture quotations in this publication, unless otherwise indicated, are from the New Revised Standard Version of the Bible, copyrighted © 1989 by the Division of Christian Education of the National Council of the Churches of Christ in the United States of America, and are used by permission.

Lessons are based on the International Sunday School Lessons for Christian Teaching, copyright © 1986, by the Committee on the Uniform Series. Text excerpted from *Adult Bible Studies,* Spring 1990.

This book is printed on acid-free, elemental chlorine-free paper.

ISBN 0-687-07438-X
ISBN-13 978-0-687-07438-9

08 09 10 11 12—10 9 8 7 6 5
Manufactured in the United States of America.

CONTENTS

Chapter One

FORGIVENESS AND FELLOWSHIP

PURPOSE

To acknowledge that forgiveness comes from Jesus Christ and that obeying his commandments enables us to have fellowship with God and with one another

BIBLE PASSAGE

1 John 1:1-10

1 We declare to you what was from the beginning, what we have heard, what we have seen with our eyes, what we have looked at and touched with our hands, concerning the word of life— 2 this life was revealed, and we have seen it and testify to it, and declare to you the eternal life that was with the Father and was revealed to us— 3 we declare to you what we have seen and heard so that you also may have fellowship with us; and truly our fellowship is with the Father and with his Son Jesus Christ. 4 We are writing these things so that our joy may be complete.

5 This is the message we have heard from him and proclaim to you, that God is light and in him there is no darkness at all. 6 If we say that we have fellowship with him while we are walking in darkness, we lie and do not do what

is true;   7 but if we walk in the light as he himself is in the light, we have fellowship with one another, and the blood of Jesus his Son cleanses us from all sin.   8 If we say that we have no sin, we deceive ourselves, and the truth is not in us. 9 If we confess our sins, he who is faithful and just will forgive us our sins and cleanse us from all unrighteousness. 10 If we say that we have not sinned, we make him a liar, and his word is not in us.

1 John 2:1-6

1 My little children, I am writing these things to you so that you may not sin. But if anyone does sin, we have an advocate with the Father, Jesus Christ the righteous;   2 and he is the atoning sacrifice for our sins, and not for ours only but also for the sins of the whole world.

3 Now by this we may be sure that we know him, if we obey his commandments.   4 Whoever says, "I have come to know him," but does not obey his commandments, is a liar, and in such a person the truth does not exist;   5 but whoever obeys his word, truly in this person the love of God has reached perfection. By this we may be sure that we are in him: 6 whoever says, "I abide in him," ought to walk just as he walked.

CORE VERSE

If we walk in the light as he himself is in the light, we have fellowship with one another, and the blood of Jesus his Son cleanses us from all sin. (1 John 1:7)

OUR NEED

The trouble had been going on for quite a while. When we were together, we spoke with civility but not with warmth. I always felt myself tighten up when he was in the room. He obviously was as sensitive to and as uncomfortable with me. It had started with a minor exchange on the telephone. It was not a large issue, just a sharp word or two. Neither of us could have felt that it amounted to anything. It was not worth mentioning, but it was keeping us tense and ill at ease.

One day he approached me, saying that we needed to talk. Still wary, I expressed surprise that we had anything to talk about. He persisted. We finally reviewed that telephone conversation, examined what had gone wrong, acknowledged our mutual errors, and parted in friendship.

After that conversation, our relationship was back to normal. Now we could talk to or ignore each other, agree or disagree; and it made no difference. Confession and forgiveness had removed the estrangement between us.

As the act of confession and forgiveness frees human relationships, it also frees us for intimate fellowship with God through Christ. We truly can be in fellowship with God only when we are free of the guilt that accompanies our failure to do God's will.

FAITHFUL LIVING

Today we begin a study entitled *Abiding in Love*. We will look at one of the most endearing parts of the New Testament, John's letters to the churches. These letters tell about love and its relationship to Christian conduct.

The letters include many of the same themes and make the same points as John's Gospel. They are the Word of God for our time as well as for the first century. They stress that we must express our faith through deeds of love rather than through the "works of the law" (Galatians 3:10).

As with many other New Testament writings, these letters appear to have been written in response to a controversy in the churches. Apparently, many churches in the first century had rival teachers and preachers. Paul spoke of them being in Corinth, and the writer of Second Peter made reference to false prophets and teachers (2 Peter 2).

We do not know what specific issues prompted the writing

of these letters. Some people simply might have wanted to start their own churches and tried to split the established churches by sowing the seeds of hatred and distrust. To these agitators John brought the word of love as well as a warning.

Some of these persons might have been claiming that confession of sin was not necessary for salvation (which would account for the emphasis on repentance) or that persons did not have to perform any Christian act of charity or that faith could be practiced without the necessity for love and mercy. Others even might have wanted to separate the love of God from a belief in Jesus Christ (a common heresy in the second century).

To these people, and others we may not know about, John, as a witness, wrote a beautifully simple yet profound introduction to the true faith: "We declare to you what we have seen and heard" (1 John 1:3).

Who are the agitators of our day, and what can you say to them that will bring healing and unity?

Do Christians Sin?

Soon after I began studying First John, I became aware that a controversy exists over whether this letter says that Christians do not sin. The dispute revolves around two separate sections of the letter. Chapters 1 and 2 appear to be a warning that we never cease sinning even if we are Christian; but Chapter 3 seems to say that if we sin at all, we have never been Christian. What is going on here?

This letter obviously was addressed to Christians; but in verse 8 of Chapter 1, we read, "If we say that we have no sin, we deceive ourselves, and the truth is not in us." That passage sounds rather conclusive; and it is supported by 2:1: "My little children, I am writing these things to you so that you may not sin. But if anyone does sin, we have an advocate with the Father, Jesus Christ the righteous." The clear implication here is that sinning is a possibility for all Christians, but restoration is available.

On the other hand, the next chapter says, "Those who have been born of God do not sin, because God's seed abides in them; they cannot sin, because they have been born of God" (1 John 3:9). The whole framework of the doctrine "once in grace, always in grace" hangs on that verse.

Some Christians, following the lead of John Wesley, the founder of Methodism, maintain that persons who have made the commitment to God still can backslide and therefore constantly need to reexamine their condition in regard to sin. Wesley held that we should be working toward perfection at all times, even though we may never reach it in this life. Other Christians claim that either those who commit sin after they are saved were never saved in the first place or their failures after they are saved are not sins.

Since it is obvious to us that we, and most of the people we know, do commit acts that are not consistent with full Christian commitment, are we to assume that no one is a Christian? How can we deal with this issue and still remain true to Scripture?

- The statement in 1 John 3:6 ("No one who abides in him sins.") may mean that people who truly are in Christ do not continue to sin. The secret is acknowledging that Christians fail to live up to the standards of Jesus Christ; but if they correct their sins as soon as they realize they are committing them, they still qualify as believers.
- First John 1 and 2 may refer to sins committed in ignorance or error, while Chapter 3 is speaking of deliberate sin. This theory could explain the distinction between "mortal sin" and "wrongdoing" in 5:16-17. It would imply that we may sin and still be Christian but that willful sin marks us as unredeemed.

• Some people may say that John is continuing the discussion in 3:2, where he says, "Beloved, we are God's children now; what we will be has not yet been revealed." He seems to imply that while we do sin now, even as Christians, we eventually will not sin if we truly abide in Christ.

I am inclined to accept the implications of all these theories. I believe that Scripture teaches that becoming Christian does not make us perfect. We must struggle daily to maintain the level of virtue that is expected of Jesus' followers. Our real test is whether we are willing to recognize and correct our sins when we discover them.

Which sins do you think are "wrongdoings," and which sins are "mortal"?

Persistence of Sin

We cannot declare that we are free of sin. We are confident, however, that when we confess our sins, we can be cleansed over and over again. Otherwise we have no hope because, as God says through John, "If we say that we have no sin, we deceive ourselves" (1 John 1:8).

These words are harsh for people who believe in the power of love, but they are not said lightly. They come from the knowledge that sin is deeply embedded in human consciousness. When we think we are living right, we may be doing wrong.

Think of the years when many people in the churches of our nation and the world did not see their racial prejudice as sin, although it clearly was against the letter and the spirit of the Scripture. Racism still may be an unseen resident in our life, preventing us from the cleansing confession that enables us to be restored fully to God. A variety of other insidious sins beguile us as well. Yet we can count on the mercy and forgiveness of God if we truly repent.

What are the most persistent sins of our time? of your life? Do you feel forgiven of all your sins? Why or why not?

Confession and Forgiveness

Confession of sin is possible only when we become aware of our sin. Our guilt may not be obvious. We do not see it until someone else tells us, and even then we tend to resist the knowledge with great vigor. Even though the Bible, from the prophets to Revelation, condemns the sin of exploiting the poor, we still do not believe we are personally involved unless it is forced to our attention.

Another difficulty is that we sometimes cannot distinguish between appropriate and inappropriate feelings of guilt. Some persons are so filled with a general sense of worthlessness that they feel guilty all the time. It is immaterial to these people whether they can identify their source of guilt or not.

Guilt is appropriate when it stems from specific acts of unrighteous behavior. It is not appropriate when it consists only of vague impressions of personal unworthiness. In order to come to confession and repentance, we need to pray that God will help us make a genuine search for our flaws.

As the forgiveness among friends restores relationships and makes them more effective in their common tasks, the forgiveness available through Jesus Christ makes us more effective Christians. Christ is the only expiation for sin, the only source of restoration and pardon. Experiencing his pardon enables us to have a more satisfying fellowship with God and with one another.

What feelings or experiences do you have when you are sure you are forgiven?

Knowing Our Sins

John gives us a way that we can know whether we are sinning or not: "We may be sure that we know him, if we obey his commandments" (1 John 2:3). That statement sounds simple, doesn't it? All we have to do to follow Jesus is to keep his commandments. But which commandments are we to follow?

The commandments of Jesus are not the same thing as the laws of Judaism or even the Ten Commandments. When John writes about the commandments of Jesus, he means that we must believe that Jesus is the Son of God; love God with all our heart, soul, and mind; and love our neighbor as our self. He carefully explains the last of these requirements in the verses that follow those in our Bible Passage: "Whoever says 'I am in the light,' while hating a brother or sister, is still in the darkness. Whoever loves a brother or sister lives in the light, and in such a person there is no cause for stumbling" (1 John 2:9-10).

These commandments are much more difficult to keep than the ones outlined in the tablets from Mount Sinai. Jesus pointed out to the rich young man that he needed to do more than observe the ten rules of living (Matthew 19:16-30). To keep the commandments of Jesus is to love God and human beings, not merely to be just or fair or to refrain from doing bodily harm. John reinforces that teaching: "Whoever says, 'I have come to know him,' but does not obey his commandments, is a liar" (1 John 2:4).

Jesus emphasized that these commandments go to the heart of human behavior. We can observe all the law and each of the Ten Commandments and still not care about anybody. We can keep the law yet have no devotion to God or to humanity. The routines of religious practice can be as deadening and as deadly as learning to swim by watching a film about swimming. We can know all the strokes but still drown.

The obedience to which God calls us in Jesus Christ is love

and service. Later John points out that we cannot claim to love until we do something for other people. "How does God's love abide in anyone who has the world's goods and sees a brother or sister in need and yet refuses help?" (1 John 3:17).

Obeying these basic commandments enables us to have fellowship with God and with one another. We cannot have one without the other. People who say they love God devoutly and claim they have turned their life over to him entirely still will be deficient unless they are committed to unconditional love for their fellow human beings.

In what ways do you fall short of keeping these commandments? What can you do about your shortcomings?

CLOSING PRAYER
O God, make us aware of our failures as people who do not obey Jesus' commandments fully. Lead us to confession and forgiveness. In Jesus' name we pray. Amen.

Chapter Two

KNOWING
AND ABIDING

PURPOSE

To accept that knowing the truth in Christ helps us avoid following false teachings

BIBLE PASSAGE

1 John 2:18-29

18 Children, it is the last hour! As you have heard that antichrist is coming, so now many antichrists have come. From this we know that it is the last hour. 19 They went out from us, but they did not belong to us; for if they had belonged to us, they would have remained with us. But by going out they made it plain that none of them belongs to us. 20 But you have been anointed by the Holy One, and all of you have knowledge. 21 I write to you, not because you do not know the truth, but because you know it, and you know that no lie comes from the truth. 22 Who is the liar but the one who denies that Jesus is the Christ? This is the antichrist, the one who denies the Father and the Son. 23 No one who denies the Son has the Father; everyone who confesses the Son has the Father also. 24 Let what you heard from the beginning abide in you. If what you heard from the beginning abides in you, then you will abide

in the Son and in the Father. 25 And this is what he has promised us, eternal life.

26 I write these things to you concerning those who would deceive you. 27 As for you, the anointing that you received from him abides in you, and so you do not need anyone to teach you. But as his anointing teaches you about all things, and is true and is not a lie, and just as it has taught you, abide in him.

28 And now, little children, abide in him, so that when he is revealed we may have confidence and not be put to shame before him at his coming.

29 If you know that he is righteous, you may be sure that everyone who does right has been born of him.

CORE VERSE
If what you heard from the beginning abides in you, then you will abide in the Son and in the Father. (1 John 2:24)

OUR NEED

Many years ago I saw my first "Christian" comic book. It had been produced by a publishing company in California and was being given away by several local groups we had begun to call the "Jesus People." They were a group of "hippies" of the sixties who had adopted a quite conservative Christian orientation and developed various communes and small groups across the country.

The comic book featured a preview of the Rapture (the end of the present age, when Christ returns), which was predicted to happen within a short time. The book presented a general sequence along with various indicators the Jesus People thought were the fulfillment of prophecy. The book also introduced the reader to people the writer considered to be false teachers, the enemies of true faith. I discovered myself among those enemies.

The first enemy had been around a long time. The book identified it as "organized religion" and used illustrations that pointed to the Roman Catholic and the Protestant traditions. Since I belonged to one of those faiths, I was clearly an enemy. The second great enemy was called the "superchurch" (which put all people who are in favor of church unity in the enemy camp). The most evil looking enemy revealed that he believed in "world brotherhood." I think I am in that group as well.

The comic book taught me that the identity of false teachers depends on who is doing the identifying. It is time that we try to learn the biblical meaning of falsehood.

FAITHFUL LIVING

In the New Testament we can find indications that not everyone knew how to tell true teachers from false. In his first letter to Corinth (Chapters 1–4), Paul seems to be saying that Apollos sometimes misrepresented the faith. In Galatians 2:11-21, Paul says that in Antioch he opposed Peter to his face. The Second Letter of Peter (3:15b-16) implies that careful reading of Paul's letters is required to keep from being misled.

To this list we may add many references to persons who went astray, led other people astray, or misrepresented some major Christian belief. At times these false teachers received quite harsh condemnation.

What we must remember is that most of these "false teachers" considered themselves to be true proponents of the Christian faith. Their views differed in some ways from the official view that finally was gathered together in the New Testament, but most of them were sincerely convinced that they had the vision of God that everyone needed in order to be a good Christian. The same is true today. Few persons who preach unacceptable doctrines are doing so with any deliberate attempt to hurt the faith. In fact, most of them genuinely feel they are helping the true faith.

I have found it difficult to accept the sincerity of people who preach a form of the gospel that is at variance with what I believe. The evidence is overwhelming, however, that a large number of sincere, well-meaning witnesses understand Scripture and Christian history quite differently from the way I understand them. These people belong to the hundreds of denominations and thousands of independent groups that exist, each of which sincerely belives that it represents the true faith. Most of these persons can quote Scripture and tradition to support their views. How can I separate the true from the false?

How do you account for the fact that so many different views of Christianity are based on the same Bible?

Who Are the False Teachers?

By now it should seem obvious that I am going to call for a great deal of tolerance for the differing views of Scripture and Christian faith. I believe that we can find arguments for tolerance of opposing views in Scripture, in Christian tradition, and in our personal experience as human beings. Without tolerance we cannot learn; and if we do not learn, we will not find ultimate truth.

Before we make tolerance our chief guide, however, we need to acknowledge that we cannot accept some philosophies as even approximations of Christian truth. We must reject them at the outset. You probably will want to make your own list, but the following are some of my choices:

- I would include all forms of totalitarianism, whether by governments or otherwise, as false teaching. I speak of systems that allow one person or group to exercise absolute power. Since we have but one God, any other agency that demands total allegiance is automatically false.
- Any form of Christian teaching that exists for the personal

enrichment of its proponents is high on my list. Those who claim to have special powers that others can obtain for a donation or who offer opportunities for support of missions that are not what they are said to be or who keep for their own use large sums of money from donations to legitimate missions are not only false but criminal. God does not trade favors for money. Anyone who offers such trades or solicits money for false missions is a swindler, even if that person or organization is draped in religious wrapping.

• Combining Christian doctrine with less acceptable ideas is particularly damaging. The tragedy of the Jim Jones cult in Guyana in 1978 shows how far that practice can go. Numerous groups gain respectability by claiming certain traditional Christian concerns while holding basic doctrines that come from sources only a little removed from superstition. These uses of Christian terminology to give credibility to nonsense are always distasteful.

• The claim that any ideology that encourages discrimination is of Christian origin is false teaching. The groups that say the Bible is the source for their bigotry are examples of this practice. Since all people are the same in God's sight, any cause that excludes others cannot be of God.

Those examples may be sufficient to make my point. Some teachings cannot be truly Christian because they deny one of the basic meanings of the faith. Many others are not so easily defined, however. John can help us find some guidelines for knowing the truth and enable us to avoid following false teaching.

Which groups or philosophies do you feel are false? Which of them are present where you live?

Knowing the Truth

In our Bible Passage and in related material from John's Gospel and the letters are hints about the nature of truth that may help us distinguish between true and false teachers:

• In the first letter John talks about "antichrists." Note the plural. We have come to think of the antichrist as a single figure who will arise in the last days. In our Bible Passage, however, John seems to equate antichrists with false teachers. They are persons who have been in the faith but have gone out on their own to preach separately (1 John 2:19). They are the opposite of the "anointed" (2:20), who have remained in fellowship with the body. Not everyone must agree on everything, but all must agree that the church is of God.

While we must be very careful not to imply that people who differ with the prevailing view of the faith are false teachers, we must recognize also that Scripture takes a dim view of freelancers. The term *anointed* denotes that some kind of approval has been granted to the people who will be teachers (apostolic succession). This idea is presented also in Second Timothy (2:2): "What you have heard from me through many witnesses entrust to faithful people who will be able to teach others as well."

Teaching is part of the body, and a person who operates outside the main body must be examined with special thoroughness. The church has a right to question persons about their adherence to commonly accepted faith interpretations and to approve them or reject them as teachers. Those who claim a personal, separate authority must demonstrate authenticity in some significant way. Their claim can be proved only when they also become part of the body.

We can say, then, that one of the guidelines First John gives us is that Christian truth comes from within the body. The one modifier is that we must be sure we know the dimensions of the body before we rush to judgment.

• A second guide is similar and comes from the same section in First John: "Let what you heard from the beginning abide in you" (2:24). The implication is that real truth has stood the test of time. The most dependable doctrines have been tested by dedicated people over many years. When some twenty-first-century person claims to have found a truth that all Christian thinkers have missed for hundreds of years, we must make a careful appraisal before we accept that claim.

Do you remember the person who discovered that the end of time was coming on September 12, 1988, and published a best-selling book (*88 Reasons Why the Rapture Will Be in 1988*, by Edgar Whisenant) about it? The buyers of the book were victims of instant truth, of which the Scripture is quite suspicious.

We must never stop learning. God continues to reveal himself to us. The Holy Spirit is a reality in all ages. Yet since the time of Jesus, we have been warned to stay with the body and to "test the spirits" (1 John 4:1) to be sure they are bringing truth instead of lies.

What personal guides do you have to help you determine the truth in Christ?

More About the Truth in Christ

John provides us with other clues about the nature of truth:

• First John 2:22 calls our attention to a guideline that is so obvious we may overlook it: "Who is the liar but the one who denies that Jesus is the Christ?" Some people in our day claim the general benefits of Christianity but fail to believe in its central tenet. It is not sufficient to offer a vision of goodness and justice without offering Christ.

Any teaching that omits this central ingredient is not the truth in Christ.

- The truth will lead persons to do right (1 John 2:29). Teaching is judged not only by its verbal accuracy but also by the effect it has on the student. We must reject any teaching that leads to behavior that is not appropriate for followers of Jesus Christ, no matter how good it sounds. Even the basic commandment of love can be twisted to encourage sexual promiscuity. Paul says in Galatians 5:13, "Only do not use your freedom as an opportunity for self-indulgence." Personal morality is a natural product of true teaching.

- True teaching always points toward love and compassion. Any doctrine that leads to hatred between persons or encourages Christians to consider themselves better than others or suggests aggression toward or exclusion of people because of who they are or how they look must be rejected.

While Christians have every right to uphold requirements of behavior and to call on believers to observe them, they have no right to impose those restrictions on others. We are warned continually not to be judgmental toward others or to abandon those persons whose faith is different from ours. The only legitimate attitude Christians can have toward fellow Christians and people outside the faith is compassion and love.

So, another guideline is that any teaching that does not express love and compassion is not worthy of Christ. Those who follow him should reject such teaching.

- A final guideline is that true Christian teaching always leads to acts of mercy and justice. "Little children, let us love, not in word or speech, but in truth and action" (1 John 3:18). It is not enough that true Christian teaching be morally, logically, or theologically correct. It also must lead to actions that express the highest ideals for the Christian community.

The theme is constant, beginning in the Old Testament with such passages as Micah 6:8: "What does the LORD require of you / but to do justice, and to love kindness, and to walk humbly with your God?" and continuing through the teachings of Jesus and into the letters of Paul and John. Doing good for others is a part of the faith. Any teaching that does not lead in that direction must be viewed critically. The truth in Christ includes acts of love, mercy, and justice.

Knowing the truth in Christ and of Christ helps us avoid false teaching. While we may not have the wisdom to judge every concept accurately when it is first presented to us, we can, through Christ, abide in the truth and prove its worth before it becomes our own. With time and the guidance of the Holy Spirit, we can know the truth; and the truth can make us free.

What is the scope of truth for you as a Christian? How does the church manifest truth?

CLOSING PRAYER
Dear God, help us apply your standards in such a way that we will know and do the truth. In Jesus' name we pray. Amen.

Chapter Three

LOVE AND HATE

PURPOSE

To emphasize that we express love best through our actions rather than through our words

BIBLE PASSAGE

1 John 3:11-21

11 For this is the message you have heard from the beginning, that we should love one another. 12 We must not be like Cain who was from the evil one and murdered his brother. And why did he murder him? Because his own deeds were evil and his brother's righteous. 13 Do not be astonished, brothers and sisters, that the world hates you. 14 We know that we have passed from death to life because we love one another. Whoever does not love abides in death. 15 All who hate a brother or sister are murderers, and you know that murderers do not have eternal life abiding in them. 16 We know love by this, that he laid down his life for us—and we ought to lay down our lives for one another. 17 How does God's love abide in anyone who has the world's goods and sees a brother or sister in need and yet refuses help?

18 Little children, let us love, not in word or speech, but

in truth and action.   19 And by this we will know that we are from the truth and will reassure our hearts before him 20 whenever our hearts condemn us; for God is greater than our hearts, and he knows everything.   21 Beloved, if our hearts do not condemn us, we have boldness before God; 22 and we receive from him whatever we ask, because we obey his commandments and do what pleases him.

23 And this is his commandment, that we should believe in the name of his Son Jesus Christ and love one another, just as he has commanded us.   24 All who obey his commandments abide in him, and he abides in them. And by this we know that he abides in us, by the Spirit that he has given us.

CORE VERSE
We know love by this, that he laid down his life for us—and we ought to lay down our lives for one another. (1 John 3:16)

OUR NEED

They were such good friends. Wherever one was, you would be sure to find the other. They had been together ever since high school. They had taken the same subjects, double dated, gone on vacations together, spent innumerable evenings talking on the phone or visiting in each other's home. Now they were in college. Betty was on a scholarship, and Margaret's education was financed by funds set aside by her wealthy father.

The first year had gone exceptionally well for Margaret. She was an outstanding scholar, a student leader; and she was popular with both faculty and students. Betty had not fared as well. Although normally she, too, was an outstanding student, worries about a parent's illness, money problems, and the breakup of a high school romance had left her exhausted and discouraged. Her grades suffered, and she had grown more and more reclusive. Betty gradually dropped her friends. By the end of the semester, she had begun to avoid Margaret.

During the summer vacation Betty got a job; and before the end of the summer, she announced that she would not be returning to college. Friends and teachers tried to talk her out of her decision, but she persisted.

Margaret, also home for the summer, became concerned about her friend. After great thought, she told her parents that she would not be returning to school, either. Over their objections, she also got a job.

During the fall Margaret resumed her friendship with Betty. When Betty's mother died, Margaret supported her friend. She encouraged Betty to maintain some of her study habits and spent time with her reviewing the first year's work. Together they made arrangements for financing the next semester; and after Christmas, Betty returned with Margaret to school.

When I talked to Betty years later, she said, "Without Margaret I don't know where I would have been. I guess I always knew that people loved me; but until Margaret put her future on the line for me, I never really believed it. She saved my life." What we do matters more than what we say.

FAITHFUL LIVING

We have ample evidence that the early churches had difficulty maintaining fellowship between their members. Squabbles broke out over differences great and small. Paul documented the problems in the church at Corinth. Disputes about honesty in giving brought fear to the whole church (Acts 5). Arguments over support for the widows of Christians led to a change in church organization (Acts 6). Disagreements about who should be allowed to go on missionary journeys created a separation (Acts 15:36-41). Concern over the matter of whether Gentiles must observe Jewish customs caused serious discussion (Acts 15:1-21).

The letters to Thessalonica speak of various failings in the church, including disrespect for pastors (1 Thessalonians 5:12) and laziness (2 Thessalonians 3:6). James seemed concerned about people who came to church to show off (2:1-13) and perhaps even worse (Chapter 4).

We should not be surprised, then, to discover that John's letters mention some of the same kinds of difficulty. As we discussed in Chapter 1, the issues seemed to center around specific persons in the congregations.

The problems of most of our congregations are not outside but inside. They involve persons and ideas that are part of that specific fellowship rather than something in the community, in the denomination, or in the world. Lack of loving fellowship in the body of Christ almost always stems from what we do to ourselves. What can we do about this problem?

What problem periods in your church have you experienced? Were you part of the problem or part of the solution?

Love and Hate

A self-study process, which some people call "Congregational Analysis," was one of the things I did in my work with local congregations. The purpose was to find out what the congregation was like so that some objectives for its future could be developed.

One of the steps in the process was to meet with the administrative council to develop a profile of the church. During the interview I asked, "If you could use one word or phrase to describe your church, what would it be?" Nearly always the first answer was, "We are a warm and caring congregation." Then I asked another question: "What does the community think of you?" Again, the first answer frequently was the same: "They think we are stuck-up and cold."

Following the two questions and answers, often a lively discussion took place about the fact that a lot of people in the church also felt that the church was cold. Next the council members arrived at the conclusion that much of the feeling of warmth existed only among those who were on the board.

We are reluctant to admit that our congregations contain both love and hate. To uncover the bad feelings, it is sometimes necessary to take drastic steps. Why?

One reason is that we do not feel that a church ought to have disagreements or disagreeable people, so we try to deny that they exist. As we can see from the review in the first section of this chapter, disputes are as much a part of the life of the church as is unity, however. Love and hate exist together.

Another reason is that we would rather not deal with our disagreements. Doing so is a long and difficult process, and often we do not have the heart for it. New pastors discover that the best way to get into trouble is to try to resolve conflicts. Often both groups turn against the pastor.

Some of us have grown discouraged because we have found that words do not always help. All the conversations, preaching, and attempts at improving interpersonal relationships do not heal the rifts.

Finally, many of us are so comfortable in our little nests in the local church that we do not want to disturb our tranquility by trying to bring the whole church together. We would rather leave it in a love/hate limbo and go about the business of enjoying our friends.

Although the members of the early church suffered the same problems as we do, they seem to have addressed them more forthrightly and to have solved them more effectively. How did they do it?

What steps has your congregation taken to resolve issues in your church? How effective were these steps?

Being by Doing

Considerable discussion has taken place in the churches over the years about the dangers in "works theology." We have heard much from both the left and the right about the necessity to believe correctly. The people who are sometimes called liberal (those who are concerned about women's rights, world peace, and racism) have joined the conservative wing (those who worry about biblical faith and witnessing) in demanding that we all get together on the right side of whatever argument. As a result, we have spent most of our energies in verbal confrontations rather than in productive work.

The writers of the New Testament did not have the fear of dealing with good deeds that some of us do. The only works that are considered undesirable in the New Testament are such ceremonial activities as circumcision, food restrictions, and so forth. Paul condemned these works throughout his letters.

In the letter to the church at Ephesus, Paul explained, "For by grace you have been saved through faith, and this is not of your own doing; it is the gift of God—not the result of works, so that no one may boast. For we are what he has made us, created in Christ Jesus for good works" (2:8-10). The works of the law, which were set up as a disciplinarian until grace appeared (Galatians 3:24), have served their purpose; but good deeds are never out of style. James said that they are inseparable from faith (2:14-26).

You may have heard that being is more important than doing. The implication is that hearts are more important than hands and that Christianity deals with who we are rather than with what we do. That expression of the faith is valid, but it is only half the story. The New Testament clearly implies that we also *are* what we *do*. The deeds of love we do for the poor and needy are as much a part of faith as our verbal expressions. One is worthless without the other. Good deeds come from faith, but faith also comes from doing good deeds. Love for God and humanity is made up of both faith and good deeds.

At what times in your life have you found that faith and works strengthened each other?

Proclaiming Love in Christ

What should our church do and be in order to be the body of Christ? That question appears to have the same answer as the question about the commandments we addressed in Chapter 1.

The local church will be more effective in overcoming problems if it will observe the two great commandments as Jesus expressed them (Matthew 22:34-40). The first responsibility of the local church is to proclaim the good news that Jesus Christ came into the world and revealed the love of God. The pulpit, the Sunday school, the women's and men's groups, the youth group, and the entire range of church activities should witness to the love of the people for God. The power of witnessing to the good news is more than conjecture. Its power has been proved over and over again in every church in every part of the world.

I had a sad experience one Sunday morning. Early in the day I listened to a dynamic minister preach against the public schools on the radio. He strongly recommended that children be enrolled in the school of the church he served as pastor. His message disturbed me. A pulpit that is used to attack the public schools, especially while serving to promote one's own school, is wasted.

A short time later I attended a church service in the city in which the church of the pastor mentioned above was located. That morning the sermon centered on peace issues. It included an impassioned defense of the "sanctuary movement" (People who are part of this movement provide shelter to persons who are escaping from political tyranny or certain death.). By the time the sermon ended, I was as put out with the use of the pulpit for this cause as I had been with the earlier one. Neither warmed my heart nor filled my soul with thanksgiving.

Thousands of topics are appropriate for sermons, but the pulpit that is not used for the proclamation of the majesty and love of God will not bring the people together.

What suggestions would you make to help your church proclaim the love of God?

Love in Action

God will not let us get by with mere verbal witness, however. John's first letter tells us that powerful words of witness are of no avail unless they are accompanied by actions. Actions are available to all of us, not only to the preacher.

John makes his point quite clear: "We know that we have passed from death to life because we love one another. Whoever does not love abides in death" (1 John 3:14). Could John have meant that heaven itself depends on affection for human beings? Apparently so, for he goes on to make his point in an unmistakable way. Not only is anyone who hates another person a murderer, John says, "How does God's love abide in anyone who has the world's goods and sees a brother or sister in need and yet refuses help? Little children, let us love, not in word or speech, but in truth and action" (3:17-18).

The church that occupies its people with ministry (showing love) will bring them into a dimension of fellowship that can transcend petty bickering. The reason we often become so intense about incidental issues is that we have never been caught up in the gospel ministry God empowers us to offer.

And God does empower us. We admire the gift of preaching, but we tend to exalt it too much. God calls us to use our gifts, practical as well as inspirational. Preaching, prophecy, and teaching are gifts; but serving, contributing, giving aid, and performing acts of mercy are gifts also (Romans 12:4-8). Paul said these gifts are "to equip the saints for the work of ministry, for building up the body of Christ" (Ephesians 4:12).

Many churches have internal strife because they have no external ministry. The secret to overcoming dissension is involving persons in forms of ministry that express their faith in such warm and personal ways that love becomes real. In action we discover what words only promise. In claiming and using our gifts of ministry, we best represent the Christ who is proclaimed from our pulpits and podiums. Proclamation and action are intertwined, but action best demonstrates the power of the gospel in the life of the people who claim Christ's name.

CLOSING PRAYER
Dear God, whose mercies are everlasting, fill us with mercy and love so that we may perform your ministry in the world. In Jesus' name we pray. Amen.

Chapter Four

FEAR AND LOVE

PURPOSE

To challenge us to love one another as God has loved us

BIBLE PASSAGE

1 John 4:7-21

7 Beloved, let us love one another, because love is from God; everyone who loves is born of God and knows God. 8 Whoever does not love does not know God, for God is love. 9 God's love was revealed among us in this way: God sent his only Son into the world so that we might live through him. 10 In this is love, not that we loved God but that he loved us and sent his Son to be the atoning sacrifice for our sins. 11 Beloved, since God loved us so much, we also ought to love one another. 12 No one has ever seen God; if we love one another, God lives in us, and his love is perfected in us.

13 By this we know that we abide in him and he in us, because he has given us of his Spirit. 14 And we have seen and do testify that the Father has sent his Son as the Savior of the world. 15 God abides in those who confess that Jesus is the Son of God, and they abide in God. 16 So we have known and believe the love that God has for us.

God is love, and those who abide in love abide in God, and God abides in them. 17 Love has been perfected among us in this: that we may have boldness on the day of judgment, because as he is, so are we in this world. 18 There is no fear in love, but perfect love casts out fear; for fear has to do with punishment, and whoever fears has not reached perfection in love. 19 We love because he first loved us. 20 Those who say, "I love God," and hate their brothers or sisters, are liars; for those who do not love a brother or sister whom they have seen, cannot love God whom they have not seen. 21 The commandment we have from him is this: those who love God must love their brothers and sisters also.

CORE VERSE

There is no fear in love, but perfect love casts out fear.
(1 John 4:18)

OUR NEED

I remember well the nights I walked home from the revival meetings we used to attend at my church in Slant, Virginia. Sometimes a lot of friends would attend, and we would engage in horseplay and shouts of laughter as we walked home. Sometimes I would be alone, which meant that I had plenty of time to remember the dire warnings voiced by the evangelist of the evening. Those warnings usually were rather graphic. Not much was left to the imagination. The fires of hell licked at my heels.

I always resented those images. They never seemed quite right as a motivation for living a life of love and service. I had discovered that discipleship was the real purpose of becoming a Christian.

By 1940, we were in a new day. New clergy came along,

and the preaching changed. Gradually we were given a more benevolent view of God and God's purposes. The emphasis was on how much God loved us and how much he wanted us to serve him through deeds of love. I made the decision to be a Christian in that atmosphere, and I found myself gladly participating in experiences of learning and growing in faith.

The fear stayed in my heart for a long time, however. Those graphic images sometimes disturbed me in the night, and I wondered if I had done enough to escape the fires. At those moments it was not service but self-preservation that made me think of God.

That attitude passed, too. Maturity brought a growing sense of the true nature of God's love and a desire to reciprocate. My desire did not always work out as well as I hoped. Like Paul, I did not always do what I wanted to do; but I did find out that the only thing God wants is for us to return and express the love he first gave us.

FAITHFUL LIVING

John's first letter is like a symphony. It weaves a few dramatic themes into the entire fabric of the writing. It does not have a rational progression from one idea to the other. They all exist side by side. We encounter the concept of love again and again. In slightly different aspects, it appears and disappears throughout the entire document. Because of that design, we will consider the subject of love in a variety of ways.

The title of this chapter is "Fear and Love," and its purpose is to find a way to describe how God's love guides our love for one another.

Fear and Love

All love relationships contain an element of fear. The reason may be that loving others makes us vulnerable. A popular song from the forties, "You Always Hurt the One You

Love," expressed that idea in romantic terms. The reverse may be equally true: The one you love always hurts you. Or, at least, we are afraid that loving may hurt us.

Our fear is justified. If you do not remember having had the following experience, you certainly know someone who did.

You are fifteen years old. You have fallen in love with great intensity. In spite of parental objections, community disapproval, or even some defect of character in the loved one, you persist in adoring him or her. If the object of your affection were to commit a crime and spend a few days in jail, your feelings might intensify. Then you learn that he or she has betrayed you in some way, perhaps by dating someone else. After investing your whole self in the relationship, you find that you feel unloved without it. The sense of loss is devastating.

The consequences of such an experience can last many years.

People in need of love depend on those who love them for their sense of self-worth. Many adults, as well as teenagers, are devastated when love is withdrawn from them at some critical moment in their life. When children turn against us or when a friendship ruptures or when divorce occurs, the results can be catastrophic. Because we know these things can happen, we may resist loving other people. We know how easy it is to get hurt.

Love can turn to hatred. We try to compensate for our loss by rejecting the person who hurt us. Some of our most intense dislikes may be the result of being disappointed over secret loves. Or if we feel we are outsiders in a social group, we may turn our hatred toward the group members.

The relationship between fear and hatred is well established in the literature of psychology. We are afraid of someone who can hurt us, either through power or by withdrawing. When our fears become a reality, they turn to hatred. The same thing can happen in faith relationships.

What memories do you have of being disappointed in love? How did you get over it?

Religion and Fear

Many religions are built on the principle that God is likely to withdraw his approval at any moment. The followers of those religions must take some steps to ensure that does not happen.

In biblical times this fear of the withdrawal of God's favor was cultivated by kings and priests, possibly for selfish purposes. Chants, dances, ceremonial dramas, and sacrifices (both animal and human) were recommended. The priest was paid for directing the dramas or received the leftovers from sacrifices. If God did not respond to that particular approach, people tended to eliminate the priests and start again. Their fear turned to hatred.

We could describe this kind of religion as an adolescent faith. It plays on teenage emotions and immature ideas. The religion Jesus brought from God is a mature faith. It does not depend on fear for its power. It offers a loving God who will do anything, including dying on a cross, to demonstrate that love. While this religion includes the teaching that people who do not choose love will endure suffering in the hereafter, its dominant theme is acceptance, forgiveness, and unending love.

The promise of free grace and unconditional love is irresistible to many people. They flock to the faith because it presents a view of God that reassures them that they will not be disappointed or abandoned. Yet some people find it impossible to leave the old ideas behind. They still think of faith as a payment for God's mercy and cannot imagine a religion that asks nothing except that they extend that love and mercy to others. They want to turn Christianity into a pagan cult, with requirements for allegiance to an angry God and blindness to human needs.

John wrote his first letter to some people like this. Over and over he told them that love is God and God is love and that the way to salvation and a life of faith is to practice love on every level and in every way. John pointed them to a view of faith that bypasses the ceremonial in favor of interpersonal affections. "In this is love, not that we loved God but that he loved us and sent his Son to be the atoning sacrifice for our sins. Beloved, since God loved us so much, we also ought to love one another" (1 John 4:10-11).

"There is no fear in love, but perfect love casts out fear. . . . We love, because he first loved us" (1 John 4:18-19). We love, not because God requires it or because it is on a list of standard responses in an order of worship, but because God led the way. The old order is gone. Sacrifices and other acts of physical penitence are of the past. God has revealed that only love counts. What God has revealed we now must share with others.

How much of your response to God is based on love, and how much is based on fear? Is that proportion changing in your life? Why or why not?

Loving Is Knowing God

We do not have to fear that God will fail us, but we need to understand what God requires of us. John tells us the basics.

"Whoever does not love does not know God, for God is love" (1 John 4:8). Love is not simply one of the nice things about God, it is God's basic character. Love has been present from the beginning and will never leave. "Love is from God; everyone who loves is born of God and knows God" (4:7).

We can forget all the other tests and dispense with codes of ethics and systematic theology. All we need to know to understand God is the meaning of love. Since God has placed love deep within the heart of all people, no one is incapable of knowing God. Only people who are afraid or who are unaware of the truth fail to realize the full potential of love through Jesus Christ.

Jesus was the perfection of love. Although love had been known always, it had never been revealed fully. At last, after people had sought for generations, Jesus Christ provided the key to the nature of God and the answer to human sin and estrangement. God loved the world enough to send his Son, asking only that humans love God and one another with the same level of affection.

Such love removes the fear that we will not have enough love. Even when the world fails to love enough, God is still love. Our dependency on love is no longer a liability but an advantage, for it leads straight to God. If we open our heart, we are sure to be among the redeemed.

That love also casts out our fear of others, for they can no longer destroy us by withholding love. Since God is love, we always have enough to spare. We can love those who do not love us, for the love of God is so powerful that it will overcome the evils humans do to one another. God protects us from the intimidation of the powerful and the ignorance of the thoughtless because God fills us with the love that removes all fear.

How does this view differ from the one that makes moral living the most important part of a Christian's life? In what ways are the two views the same?

Applying Love

My friend Ray Gibson preached a sermon asking people to imagine they were again children who needed to understand the meaning of love. It is summarized below:

• We would not want to possess an "if" love. "If" love is always conditional. It promises that we will have plenty of love if we meet certain conditions: if we play a good game of football, if we study hard, if we have a successful career, or if we marry the right person. "If" love keeps everyone on edge. It constantly calls everyone to judgment. "If" love brings no rest.

• We would not want to possess a "because" love. "Because" love is a product of something: I love you because you are pretty, because you are from a good family, or because you have a high IQ. This kind of love is depressing. Since we cannot help what we are (plain, from a lower-income family, of modest intelligence), we can never be loved. Even people who have these advantages sometimes fear they may lose them, and then no one will love them.

• We want love to be "anyhow," which is God's love. God's love says, "Well, you didn't make the team; but I love you anyhow" or, "Even if you won't be at the top of your class, I love you." God's love means, "I see you have quite a problem, but I love you anyhow." God's love does not expect perfection or accomplishment beyond our ability; it simply offers to love us anyhow, no matter what the circumstances.

God offers us "anyhow" love, and he expects us to offer that kind of love to others.

How do we apply this kind of love? John said that we must love our fellow human beings always. If we cannot love other people, we cannot love God. We are to love everyone, with no exceptions. When we are able to love others, we will know what the love of God really means.

Jesus said, "If you love those who love you, what reward do you have? Do not even the tax collectors do the same? And if you greet only your brothers and sisters, what more are you doing than others? Do not even the Gentiles do the same? Be perfect, therefore, as your heavenly Father is perfect" (Matthew 5:46-48).

The practical application of the gospel of Jesus Christ overcomes the barriers to love that ages of human practice have set up. The gospel is so powerful because it calls us to that ideal. It remains unfulfilled because most of us have not yet achieved the measure of love that will express in our world what God has done for us by his love.

All people have a need for love and a need to love. We are never complete until we learn to give and to receive love. Receiving sometimes is the harder for us. We must offer love; but we must be willing to receive it as well, both from God and from others. The Scriptures help us understand that we cannot give the love God asks us to express until we have accepted the love God has for us. When we accept God's love, we can meet the challenge to love one another as he has loved us.

CLOSING PRAYER

God of love, make us loving, too, that we may feel the power of love and know its joy in all we do. In Jesus' name we pray. Amen.

Chapter Five

FAITH AND LIFE

PURPOSE

To show that faith in Jesus Christ alters our way of living and gives us eternal life

BIBLE PASSAGE

1 John 5:1-13

1 Everyone who believes that Jesus is the Christ has been born of God, and everyone who loves the parent loves the child.   2 By this we know that we love the children of God, when we love God and obey his commandments.   3 For the love of God is this, that we obey his commandments. And his commandments are not burdensome,   4 for whatever is born of God conquers the world. And this is the victory that conquers the world, our faith.   5 Who is it that conquers the world but the one who believes that Jesus is the Son of God?

6 This is the one who came by water and blood, Jesus Christ, not with the water only but with the water and the blood. And the Spirit is the one that testifies, for the Spirit is the truth.   7 There are three that testify: 8 the Spirit and the water and the blood, and these three agree. 9 If we receive human testimony, the testimony of God is

greater; for this is the testimony of God that he has testified to his Son.   10 Those who believe in the Son of God have the testimony in their hearts. Those who do not believe in God have made him a liar by not believing in the testimony that God has given concerning his Son.   11 And this is the testimony: God gave us eternal life, and this life is in his Son.   12 Whoever has the Son has life; whoever does not have the Son of God does not have life.

13 I write these things to you who believe in the name of the Son of God, so that you may know that you have eternal life.

CORE VERSE

This is the testimony: God gave us eternal life, and this life is in his Son. (1 John 5:11)

OUR NEED

I have come to believe that heredity is a powerful force and that much of our behavior is the result of our genes. Yet I run into evidence all the time that everything is not fixed and that people can change. A good example was my Uncle Bill.

Uncle Bill came to my parents' home when he was in his late nineties, prepared to live out his life with us. What I did not mention was that we had lived with him earlier. I will never forget the four years we lived on his farm in Idaho.

At that time, Uncle Bill was getting a divorce. He had married at forty-two. After twenty years of marriage, he had decided that he could not stand it anymore. In those days, it was necessary to set up residence in Reno, Nevada to get a quicky divorce. So we stayed on the farm while he went to Reno. Then we stayed on for a few years after he returned. They were not happy years because Uncle Bill had a mean streak. Finally, we moved back to Virginia.

A little later we heard that Uncle Bill had married again. His new wife was an acquaintance from our days in Idaho. Her husband had died, and she and Uncle Bill decided to marry. From what we could hear, it was a happy match; but we only saw them together once. When she died and Uncle Bill came to live with us, the whole family wondered how we would put up with the mean old man we remembered.

Imagine our surprise. He was thoughtful, genteel, and an absolute delight. We could hardly believe it. When we found the nerve to ask him about this change, he said, "Thirty-three years with the right woman makes a man a different person."

Right relationships change people. Our relationship with Jesus Christ changes us most.

FAITHFUL LIVING

After using almost his entire first letter to talk about the value of loving persons as evidence of the love of God, John included a statement about the importance of loving God in learning to love other persons: "By this we know that we love the children of God, when we love God and obey his commandments" (1 John 5:2).

Perhaps John realized that he might be giving the wrong impression by talking so much about love for humans. He makes sure that the readers have their priorities clearly arranged by reminding them that loving God is the first step in the new life. Being born of God through faith is the changing force. All the rest flows from that. "This is the victory that overcomes the world, our faith" (1 John 5:4).

The introduction of this way of stating the truth that Jesus came to reveal completes the picture. Although it is quite difficult to say which is more important in proving the other, loving God and loving persons are strongly interrelated. We cannot omit either approach.

Three evidences of God are at work in the world. We need to look briefly at them.

What reaction do you have to John's restatement of the impor-tance of loving? Does it help, hurt, confuse, or clarify?

The Testimony of Witnesses

Most Bible commentaries remind us that Jewish law requires three witnesses to establish evidence. If two witnesses disagree, the third can settle the issue. This legal practice may be the background for the statement here about three witnesses who agree on the meaning of the coming of Jesus (1 John 5:7-8).

The entire passage (1 John 5:6-11) is about witness. One expert has pointed out that the Greek word for *witness* or *testimony* is used nine times in these six verses. John probably is making sure he communicates the point about the reality of the Christ.

John concentrates on the testimony of God because it is the greatest proof. People who have heard that testimony will believe. Those who have not heard that testimony will not believe, even if they hear many human testimonies. To settle the argument, he speaks of three witnesses: the Spirit, the water, and the blood:

• The Spirit is, of course, the inward witness. It speaks to the heart. That witness might be likened to the moment when hands are laid on pastors at their ordination, just as the dove symbolizing the Spirit was a witness at the baptism of Jesus.
• The water is the symbol of cleansing through baptism. It is the witness of membership in the body of Christ. It repre-sents the unity of the faith, which is itself a powerful wit-ness. It publicly declares whose side we are on.
• The blood refers to the death of Jesus on the cross, which was the supreme act that freed us from sin. It is a symbol of the change that occurs in the life of each person who con-

fesses Christ as Lord. The Lord's Supper particularly points to this witness. Each time we share the cup, we witness anew to the power of God through Christ.

These witnesses are the ones to believe, for "those who believe in the Son of God have the testimony in their hearts" (1 John 5:10). We need not depend on frail human beings to convince us of the truth of God. That truth is verified in us through these three witnesses. God is speaking to us through each of them.

What witness do you find the most convincing in proving the reality of Christ?

Modes of Loving God

We do not always find it easy to love God in appropriate ways. We can comprehend loving others as a way of showing God's love for us, but the ways of expressing love for and to God are not so clear.

More than one writer has described this process as using all of our modes of being in response to God. Using the three-part division of personality from traditional sources, they examine each part for clues about how we may love God from the totality of our being.

• *Thinking.* The first division is the intellect: loving God with the mind. For some people, thinking is the most effective way because it is the way they process information about the world around them.

Thinking people tend to become scholars and theologians who try to understand the nature of God and the world. Seeing God as the Creator; recounting the story of God's relationship with the earth and its inhabitants; searching for clues about how God works in the world; exploring the great works of the mind, including Scripture; trying to find and appreciate the principles of the natural order; and other rational pursuits are effective ways of expressing our admiration and affection for God.

Thinkers express love in more formal ways. Sometimes they almost seem detached, but they make it possible for some of the rest of us to know more about the natural world and God's part in it.

Loving God changes our way of thinking. Where once rationality was an end in itself, it now becomes an instrument we may use to help us understand God. Creative expression, which often is used for personal advantage, becomes a way of glorifying God. For the love of God we conduct research, write books, compose music, and develop medical processes for the benefit of humankind. The pursuit of learning becomes the pursuit of the knowledge of God.

The scientific work of Albert Schweitzer in Africa or Marie Curie in France, the astronomy of Fred Hoyle, the theology of Thomas Aquinas or Georgia Harkness, and the books by C. H. Lewis are products of the rational mind that is set on God.

• *Feeling.* Some people are more tuned to the senses than to the intellect. Their basic mode of relating to the world is through awareness of moods and relationships. They are inclined toward emotional rather than rational processes. The plight of others affects them, and they feel deeply the impact of natural beauty. Truth affects them as a passion rather than as a conviction. They cry, laugh, and feel joy more keenly than others.

Feeling people tend to work in the helping professions: nurses, counselors, poets, or social workers. When the love of God becomes their goal, they become Frank Lauback, teaching the world to read; Mother Teresa, working in the slums of Calcutta; or Fanny Crosby, expressing faith through the poetry of the people. They open Christian community centers and protect the environment for the glory of God. Loving God changes the ways people express feelings.

• *Acting.* The will, or the decision-making process, is a third component of the traditional view of personality. People in this area are inclined to do something. Rather than spending a lot of time analyzing information (thinking) or reacting to it (feeling), they quickly formulate decisions and make a strong commitment to action.

These people start business enterprises or community agencies or work in highly self-directed occupations. When motivated by the desire to express love to God, they may become determined to spread the gospel throughout the world.

How does the dominant part of your personality (thinking, feeling, or acting) affect your faith experience?

Changes, Changes!
Loving God does not change the personality of people. We may continue to be the way we are throughout our life. Yet when the love of God enters a person's life, some things do change.

• *Motives change.* The forces that impel action come from a person's spiritual center rather than from personal ambition or enlightened self-interest.
• *Perspectives change.* As rivers look different from their banks than they do from an airplane flying overhead, so the events of an age look different through the eyes of faith than they do through the eyes of those who are using them for selfish purposes.
• *Behavior changes.* Ethical and moral considerations that

come from God, rather than from current fads, determine what a person does.

• *Evaluations change.* Projects are valued according to their worth to the kingdom of God rather than for their potential for personal gain or acclaim.

Faith in Jesus Christ and the love of God changes us. After we know God, things are never the same. Life may not be as dramatically different for us as it has been for some, but the love of God will conspicuously or subtly alter what we are and what we do.

In what ways have you changed since you confessed Christ as Lord?

The Products of Faith

Faith produces new life. We already knew that, but the words in Chapter 5 of First John provide a new way of expressing that new life. We might call these phrases the *products of faith.*

• *We receive confirmation that we are children of God.* "Everyone who believes that Jesus is the Christ has been born of God" (1 John 5:1). We have always been children of God. We were made by God, who numbered every hair on our head. We are worth more than many sparrows, and God looks out for us day and night. The impact of God's parenthood takes on new meaning for us when we discover the presence of God through faith. Before we were as children who know they have a parent somewhere; now we know God as an intimate presence. The Spirit of God dwells with us, and we walk in the light of his presence.

• *We discover the commandments as a guide for life.* We have always had moral guidance and rules to live by. Even the most secular people have those resources. It is possible to be a good person without knowing Jesus Christ. Knowing

Christ makes a great difference, however. The commandments we have explored in these chapters are dynamic
reminders of the core of life. They give us a way to imbue
our existence with meaning and significance. "His commandments are not burdensome," John reminds us
(1 John 5:3). They are the basic pathways to a productive life.

- *We discover strength to overcome the world.* The world is with us
  always. While we can keep it under control by force of will
  for a while, it will get to us eventually unless we have
  resources beyond ourselves on which we can call. The power
  of God through faith enables us to deal constructively with
  the world as it is. The ability to put the world in proper per-
  spective is one of the most beneficial products of faith.

- *We find inner resources.* "Those who believe in the Son of
  God have the testimony in their hearts" (1 John 5:10). All
  the resources of philosophy, science, and mathematics
  cannot prove that God is real. The presence of God in the
  human heart is the only proof that counts.

- *We anticipate eternal life.* Eternal life is a promise. As Christians
  we cannot count on special treatment in this life, but we can
  expect all sorts of spiritual rewards. This world has injustice
  we cannot resolve and unfinished tasks we cannot complete.
  Only in the world to come will all be resolved. In faith we can
  be confident of participating in the perfect eternity.

These products of faith are part of the joy of being in
Christ. They alter our way of living and give us eternal life.

CLOSING PRAYER
We are confident, O God, that life with you will be
abundant. Give us the will to be in faith that we may live
in you. In Jesus' name we pray. Amen.

6

Chapter Six

LOYALTY AND DISCIPLESHIP

PURPOSE

To discover that loyalty to Jesus Christ includes deeds of love and mercy

BIBLE PASSAGE

2 John 1-6

1 The elder to the elect lady and her children, whom I love in the truth, and not only I but also all who know the truth,   2 because of the truth that abides in us and will be with us forever:

3 Grace, mercy, and peace will be with us from God the Father and from Jesus Christ, the Father's Son, in truth and love.

4 I was overjoyed to find some of your children walking in the truth, just as we have been commanded by the Father. 5 But now, dear lady, I ask you, not as though I were writing you a new commandment, but one we have had from the beginning, let us love one another.   6 And this is love, that we walk according to his commandments; this is the commandment just as you have heard it from the beginning— you must walk in it.

3 John 1:1-8
1 The elder to the beloved Gaius, whom I love in truth.

2 Beloved, I pray that all may go well with you and that you may be in good health, just as it is well with your soul. 3 I was overjoyed when some of the friends arrived and testified to your faithfulness to the truth, namely how you walk in the truth. 4 I have no greater joy than this, to hear that my children are walking in the truth.

5 Beloved, you do faithfully whatever you do for the friends, even though they are strangers to you; 6 they have testified to your love before the church. You will do well to send them on in a manner worthy of God; 7 for they began their journey for the sake of Christ, accepting no support from non-believers. 8 Therefore we ought to support such people, so that we may become co-workers with the truth.

CORE VERSE

Beloved, you do faithfully whatever you do for the friends, even though they are strangers to you. (3 John 5)

OUR NEED

Approaching the end of writing this book brings both relief and sadness. By the time I finish writing a book on the Scriptures, the material seems like a familiar friend, comfortable and reassuring. Writing a book never fails to inform, challenge, and gratify me. The opportunity to study the Bible and to share the results of that study with a wide range of readers gives me great pleasure.

Still, I usually come to the end with a vague sense of unease. After all that work and all those words, will anything happen that makes a difference in the life of the people who will read these chapters? Do we enter God's Word in order to find some comforting phrases and a happy ending, or is our purpose to find motivation for our life? Have I written in such a way that persons can discover how they can put the gospel into practice?

I do not mean to say that study is unimportant or useless. We constantly need the refreshment of the mind and heart through renewal of the ties with Scripture and tradition. Inquiry and reflection are part of the foundation of Christian maturity. Yet I am aware that God calls us to the world beyond the academic.

John keeps telling us that loving God means doing something for other persons. He gives the process of devotional study little attention. When John is God's spokesperson, we hear a trumpet call to action. Christians express their loyalty to Christ by deeds rather than by words.

FAITHFUL LIVING

Unlike John's first letter, the two we are studying in this chapter appear to be addressed to specific readers. Second John begins with the phrase, "The elder to the elect lady and her children." The third letter is addressed "to the beloved Gaius." In each case John adds the phrase, "whom I love in the truth" or "in truth," which may be a common salutation such as "grace, mercy, and peace." Who received these letters?

The "elect lady" is quite mysterious. With her children, some of whom follow the truth (and apparently some of whom do not), she would appear to be a familiar leader in the fellowship. However, an air of formality in the salutation makes many commentators feel that the lady really is the church in the community that received the letter and her children are its members. While "elect lady" may seem to be a strange way to address a church, it is not unprecedented.

Gaius, on the other hand, seems to be a real person.

We even have a hint that he was one of John's close supporters, to whom John turned when he discovered that Diotrephes (3 John 9) no longer accepted his authority. Diotrephes probably was a major church officer who had decided to take matters into his own hands.

Whoever received the letters, they clearly are written from the same point of view as John's first letter. They carry some of the same themes and communicate the same message. Love, commandments, and truth are coupled with a warning against those who deceive the church with false teaching.

The Dynamics of Loyalty

Loyalty was a particularly valuable trait in the early church. The church had few workers, and those who could be counted on were quite valuable. The new fellowship of Christians needed strong leaders who had great fidelity to the teachings of Jesus and the early followers. In addition, danger existed in all directions. Disloyalty placed everyone at risk.

In that environment the Christian community considered disloyal people to be lost. John, in his first letter, cast doubt on the ability of anyone to return to the faith who deliberately departed. Some of Paul's letters and the Book of Revelation echo his idea. Jesus anticipated this sin that later was to be called "apostasy" (leaving or renouncing the faith): "No one who puts a hand to the plow and looks back is fit for the kingdom of God" (Luke 9:62).

Disloyalty had serious consequences. The Letter to the Hebrews is quite graphic: "Anyone who has violated the law of Moses dies without mercy 'on the testimony of two or three witnesses.' How much worse punishment do you think will be deserved by those who have spurned the Son of God . . . and outraged the Spirit of grace?" (10:28-29). Although moral failings were deplored, and all the New Testament witnesses condemned pride and covetousness, these sins were not considered as bad as apostasy.

The reason is clear. Since no written documents existed and principles of the faith lived only in the hearts of Christ's followers, keeping the purity of the faith intact was very important. Good teachers were highly prized, and poor ones were condemned.

The reaction to apostasy was so bitter that some scholars feel that it was the "unforgivable sin." In any case, apostasy clearly was the worst failing of the Christian. The entire church shared the contempt of the leaders for those who abandoned the truth.

Who are the apostates in the church today? What could you do to help them?

The Answer to Apostasy

John, as much as anyone, detested people who were disloyal to the faith. He shared with his readers all the bitterness and much of the desire for expulsion and punishment. His approach to the prevention of apostasy was a little different, however. He gave us a clearer word of God about the matter, possibly, than we can find anywhere else in Scripture.

John returned to this original theme in both his second and third letters. He said, "This is love, that we walk according to his commandments; this is the commandment just as you have heard it from the beginning—you must walk in it" (2 John 6). This is the secret to promoting loyalty among members of the church. The third letter is even more specific: "Beloved, you do faithfully whatever you do for the friends, even though they are strangers to you" (3 John 5). Nothing will prevent apostasy as successfully as the practice of love, both as an emotion and as an act of support and comfort. Loyalty to Christ finds its best expression in the relationships of love.

How would you define loyalty to Christ? In what ways do you exhibit these characteristics?

The Glue of the Fellowship

The local church lives or dies on deeds of love and mercy. Any other foundation eventually erodes, leaving the congregation with a decline in both morale and membership. John showed that he understood this fact when he put love and service at the top of the list of qualities for good church members.

Modern studies confirm this observation. Church growth literature uniformly asserts that the attractiveness of a church to prospective new members depends more on the image of loving care it projects than on anything else. Some people are attracted by a dynamic pulpiteer, some attend for the variety of program offerings, and a few join because of some imagined social benefit. But most people judge the quality of a church by the quality of its care and concern for its members.

Large and small churches are not different. We judge them all in the same way. The only difference is that small membership churches think they are more loving, even if they are not. It is not enough to have a small core of persons who are fond of one another. They must also reach out especially to strangers beyond the inner circle.

The components of love and mercy in a local congregation include regularly greeting visitors, visiting of both members and prospects by church members (in addition to pastoral visits), having regularly planned activities for fellowship and support, and paying special attention to people who have special needs (members of all ages who are confined to their home, persons with disabling conditions, people who are in threatening economic circumstances, victims of disasters, and anyone who suffers from some form of discrimination).

While these activities may seem routine, they are the most neglected areas in most churches. In numerous studies of the long-range needs of the local church, I discovered that if churches would follow the advice contained in John's letters and initiate a competent "caring program," they could improve their prospects for growth and effectiveness. When the local church becomes the center for acts of love and mercy, its long-range needs will take care of themselves.

How well does your church do in performing acts of love and mercy? What other programs could you help initiate?

Reaching Out in Love and Mercy

Throughout the discussion of the meaning of love and mercy, John keeps reminding us that Christian expectations are modeled on the example of Jesus. One of the characteristics of Jesus' ministry was that he reached out to people who were beyond the core fellowship. The poor, the rich young man, a woman accused of adultery, a mentally disturbed man, people of other nations and races—all were recipients of his attention and care. If we are to be like Jesus, we also must be involved beyond the doors of the church.

John specifically reminds us that such care begins with the people who carry the gospel to other places: "We ought to support such people, so that we may become co-workers with the truth" (3 John 8). People who work in and for the church deserve the best care the church can give, even if they are strangers to the local congregation. Not only John's letters but other parts of the New Testament strongly recommend that the local church extend its love and care to those who work on its behalf. The early church provided this care through hospitality and special offerings.

The community around the church is one of the best areas for outreach. Hardly a community exists that does not have persons who are hungry and unclothed, lonely and isolated, and who need the affirmation of Christian love. Protestant churches in some areas tend to attract people of similar social standing and tragically ignore the people in the community who are different from the majority of the church's members.

Acts of love and mercy include establishing schools, hospitals, homes, and agencies for social service. Ministry involves fighting social evils such as abuse of alcohol and other drugs, the exploitation of workers, child pornography, racism, ageism, and sexism.

Love and mercy also include extending our concern to the whole world. With modern-day communication, transportation, and commercial exchange, we are becoming more of a single unit than we have ever been. What affects one of us affects all of us.

Some people question the church's involvement in global concerns and attempt to discourage personal and financial support. It is ironic that as we are becoming one world, some people want to withdraw from world mission and ministry. These Christian isolationists have forgotten that Jesus drew no boundaries. We can place no limits on the deeds of love and mercy in a church that seeks to practice loyalty to the vision of ministry Jesus Christ established.

What would you say to people who want to restrict the ministry of the church to the areas of evangelism and spiritual growth for members only?

The Whole Ministry of God

The New Testament makes a persistent effort to help us understand what the new faith requires of people who would follow Christ. Since the early Christians had seen nothing like it before, evangelists, writers, and local church leaders constantly interpreted the new faith to all believers.

We are fortunate indeed that God guided his people to collect the writings that reflected his true word and to keep them safe for our enlightenment. Through God's action, we may know the truth that will make us free.

John's letters introduce us to the heart of the ministry: the manifestation of the love of God as revealed in Jesus. When fully implemented, this ministry of love becomes the gospel for the whole world.

CLOSING PRAYER

O God, your care for us includes the provision of your Word for our time. Bring us to a new appreciation of the depth and height of your love. In Jesus' name we pray. Amen.